My Emotions
Mis emociones

BORED
ABURRIDO

A Crabtree Roots Book
Un libro de Las Raíces de Crabtree

AMY CULLIFORD
Traducción de Pablo de la Vega

Crabtree Publishing
crabtreebooks.com

School-to-Home Support for Caregivers and Teachers

This book helps children grow by letting them practice reading. Here are a few guiding questions to help the reader with building his or her comprehension skills. Possible answers appear here in red.

Before Reading:

- What do I think this book is about?
    - *This book is about feeling bored.*
    - *This book is about what feeling bored looks or feels like.*

- What do I want to learn about this topic?
    - *I want to learn what makes people feel bored.*
    - *I want to learn what feeling bored looks like.*

During Reading:

- I wonder why...
    - *I wonder why we yawn when we are bored.*
    - *I wonder what we can do when we are bored.*

- What have I learned so far?
    - *I have learned that you can read if you are bored.*
    - *I have learned that you can play a game if you are bored.*

After Reading:

- What details did I learn about this topic?
    - *I have learned that it is okay to feel bored.*
    - *I have learned that there are many things you can do when you feel bored.*

- Read the book again and look for the vocabulary words.
    - *I see the word **rains** on page 4 and the word **yawn** on page 6. The other vocabulary words are found on page 14.*

I am **bored**.

Estoy **aburrida**.

I am bored when it **rains**.

Me aburro cuando **llueve**.

I **yawn** when I am bored.

Bostezo cuando estoy aburrido.

I am bored in the **car**.

Cuando voy en el **automóvil** me aburro.

I **read** when I am bored.

Leo cuando estoy aburrido.

I play a **game** when I am bored.

Juego cuando estoy aburrido.

When do you feel bored?

¿Cuándo te sientes aburrido?

Words to Know
Palabras para conocer

bored
aburrida

car
automóvil

game
juego

rains
llueve

read
leo

yawn
bostezo

40 Words

I am **bored**.

I am bored when it **rains**.

I **yawn** when I am bored.

I am bored in the **car**.

I **read** when I am bored.

I play a **game** when I am bored.

When do you feel bored?

29 palabras

Estoy **aburrida**.

Me aburro cuando **llueve**.

Bostezo cuando estoy aburrido.

Cuando voy en el **automóvil** me aburro.

Leo cuando estoy aburrido.

Juego cuando estoy aburrido.

¿Cuándo te sientes aburrido?

My Emotions

BORED

Mis emociones

ABURRIDO

Written by: Amy Culliford

Designed by: Rhea Wallace

Series Development: James Earley

Proofreader: Ellen Rodger

Educational Consultant: Marie Lemke M.Ed.

Photographs:
Shutterstock: Juan Pablo Gonzaález: cover; diplomedia: p. 1; Syda Productions: p. 3, 14; GOLFX: p. 5, 14; airdone: p. 7, 14; Leszek Glasner: p. 8-9, 14; Zurijeta: p. 10, 14; Motortion Films: p. 11, 14; fizkes: p. 13

Crabtree Publishing

crabtreebooks.com 800-387-7650

Printed in Canada/052023/CPC20230516

Published in Canada
Crabtree Publishing
616 Welland Ave.
St. Catharines, Ontario
L2M 5V6

Published in the United States
Crabtree Publishing
347 Fifth Avenue,
Suite 1402-145
New York, NY, 10016

Library and Archives Canada Cataloguing in Publication
Available at the Library and Archives Canada

Library of Congress Cataloging-in-Publication Data
Available at the Library of Congress

Paperback: 9781039624504
Ebook: 9781039625341
Epub: 9781039624924